KT-172-640

OTHER HELEN EXLEY GIFTBOOKS IN THIS SERIES:

A Feast of After Dinner Jokes   Over 30s' Jokes
A Portfolio of Business Jokes   A Spread of Over 40s' Jokes
A Megabyte of Computer Jokes   A Triumph of Over 50s' Jokes
A Century of Cricket Jokes   A Jubilee of Over 60s' Jokes
A Binge of Diet Jokes   A Knockout of Sports Jokes
A Round of Golf Jokes   A Bouquet of Wedding Jokes
A Romp of Naughty Jokes

Published simultaneously in 1999 by Helen Exley Giftbooks Ltd in
Great Britain, and Helen Exley Giftbooks LLC in the USA.
Selection and arrangement copyright © Helen Exley 1999
Text copyright © Stuart and Linda Macfarlane 1999
Cartoons copyright © Bill Stott 1999
The moral rights of the authors have been asserted.

20 19 18 17 16 15 14 13

Written by Stuart and Linda Macfarlane.
Cartoons by Bill Stott.
Edited by Claire Lipscomb.
Series Editor: Helen Exley.

ISBN 1-86187-124-4

A copy of the CIP data is available from the British Library on request.
All rights reserved. No part of this publication may be reproduced or
transmitted in any form or by any means, electronic or mechanical,
including photocopy, recording or any information storage and
retrieval system without permission in writing from the publisher.
Printed in China.

Helen Exley Giftbooks Ltd, 16 Chalk Hill, Watford, Herts WD19 4BG, UK.
Helen Exley Giftbooks LLC, 185 Main Street, Spencer, MA 01562, USA.
www.helenexleygiftbooks.com

OLD WRECKS' JOKES

BY STUART & LINDA MACFARLANE

CARTOONS BY BILL STOTT

A HELEN EXLEY GIFTBOOK

Signs that you're an old wreck

- Your birth certificate is written in roman numerals.

- Archaeologists dig up things you remember from your childhood.

- You are entering your fourth childhood.

- You remember a time when you could fix the television by giving it a good thump.

- A trip down memory lane requires a map.

- Your best-loved music is only available on 33 RPM vinyl.

- Even people you don't know call you Grandad/Grandma.

- Children ask you if you ever had a dinosaur for a pet.

"HEY! NOSE HAIR! I'M THAT OLD?"

Gripes and grumbles

When you're an oldie there is no need to feel miserable on your birthday – just smile and forget all about your advancing age, rheumatism, lumbago....

In old age happiness is a state of mind best created by causing misery to someone else.

"IN THE SEVENTIES YOU WERE AN ENGAGING GRUMBLER.... TWENTY YEARS ON YOU'VE BECOME A TEDIOUS MOANER...."

If you think life at eighty is really miserable – just wait till you are ninety.

Frustrated with friends continually moaning about old age? Insist that they make a note of any available alternative to old age.

The worse for wear

Old age is when you nap between sleeps.

You know that you are an oldie when you need to use a hammer to open cans and jars.

Old age is when you have bunions on your bunions.

A new doctor had been assigned to the retirement home and she asked Maisie how she was feeling.

"My legs ache, I can hardly move my hands, I constantly have chest pains..."

"That's awful" said the doctor, "I had better give you a thorough examination."

"That won't be necessary," said Maisie abruptly, "you don't understand – I haven't felt as good as this for years!"

"IS THAT ENTIRELY NECESSARY GRANDAD? IT'S ONLY A STAIR-LIFT!"

Lie, lie, lie again

As you move into the autumn of life remember that age is an art not a science – there is no need to be precise.

When asked, round your age down to the nearest decade.

How to pass for fifty-nine

Keep "Happy fifty-ninth birthday" cards in prominent places.

Develop the habit of starting every sentence with "I'm fifty-nine you know!"

Buy all your friends cameras which are fitted with soft focus lenses.

Only ever go out on a dark night.

Lie, lie, lie again.

"DOES IT MAKE YOU LOOK YOUNGER? NO. IT MAKES
YOU LOOK LIKE AN EIGHTY-ONE YEAR OLD IN LYCRA
SHORTS AND A DAFT HELMET."

Courting for old codgers

For those who have not been part of the dating game for many years, here are a few rules and tips.

Top three pick-up joints for oldies
1. At the large print section of the library.
2. By the dental adhesive stand at the drugstore.
3. Rummaging through the sale items in the thermal underwear department.

Where to go: A candlelit restaurant is good camouflage. Choose one which plays background music – this will help drown out the slurping noises.

Kissing: This should never be done unless both parties have their false teeth in.

Time to go home: Remember, you and your partner are no longer youngsters – so, what the hell, stay out all night if you want.

"YOU DIRTY OLD DEVIL! BY THE WAY, THERE ARE
TWO 'T'S IN 'BUTTOCK'."

The memory's the first to go...

Joe arrived home from a shopping trip to the supermarket. As his wife checked through the groceries she complained that he had forgotten many of the items he was supposed to buy. "At least I remembered to drive home in the car this time," announced Joe with an air of satisfaction. "Car! What car? We don't own a car!" shrieked his wife.

Old mother Hubbard
Went to the cupboard
To fetch her poor dog a bone
But when she got there
She forgot why she'd gone
So she made
herself a nice
pot of tea.

"GERRY'S ALWAYS BEEN VERY FUSSY ABOUT HIS
APPEARANCE... PITY ABOUT HIS MEMORY."

An advanced case of nostalgia

Reminiscing: The art of combining fact with fiction to produce fantasy.

What are the "good old days"? They are those days, far in the past, which your memory is unable to recall completely or accurately. To compensate, the brain fills in all the blanks with a random selection from the "Happy Bank" section of its filing system.

In the good old days...

... today's antiques were available new.

... you could warm your hands on the radio.

... knees were shocking.

... fashion models were not constructed of silicon.

... old people seemed much older than they do now!

"YOU JUST CAN'T GET A DECENT PICTURE THESE DAYS..."

Miracles of science

Due to advances in technology,
people are living to a much greater age
than ever before. Now the stages of growing
older are termed Middle Age, Old Age and
Synthetic Age.

As you age, your sight deteriorates requiring a
growth in spectacle strength.
In the beginning there are spectacles.
Next come bifocals. These are replaced
by trifocals then quadfocals.
Octafocals give way to multifocals, until
your spectacles have so many facets
that they resemble the eyes of flies.

Dentists are now able to supply sets of completely natural-looking false teeth – yes, half the teeth are complete with fillings, and the other half appear to be in an advanced stage of decay.

It's so ironic. The human race has the technology to travel to the moon. But we have failed miserably in developing a wig that can't be detected by a short-sighted moron from the other side of a darkened room.

Fond memories

Oldies' maxim on sex 1: One benefit of a poor memory is that you can convince yourself that you have had sex recently but have just forgotten.

Oldies' maxim on sex 2: The memories are better than the activity ever was.

"ARE YOU SEEING SOMEONE ELSE?"

Oldie sex: A mystical activity which occasionally makes fleeting appearances into dreams.

How to get your
own way

- Pretend to be confused by new technology.

- Sit in your armchair and use everyone around you as your remote control.

- Use the threat of moving in with your children to get them to do all your shopping and housework.

- Let everyone know that only your nicest relatives will be rewarded in your will.

- Feign illness whenever you need anything done.

"BIRTHDAY? I'VE ALREADY HAD EIGHTY-FOUR OF THOSE
DARLIN'S – I EXPECT THIS'LL BE MY LAST...."

Old wrecks' quiz

Determine how old you really are!

1. How attractive are you to the opposite sex?

a) I have a constant stream of admirers.

b) A secret admirer once sent me a card.

c) People turn away as I walk down the street.

2. When you see your body in the mirror what do you think?

a) I'm living proof that youth can be eternal.

b) I look good for a ninety year old. It's a pity that I'm only sixty-three.

c) Help! I've turned into a dinosaur.

3. How good is your memory?

a) I can remember the day I was born.

b) I can remember all the days of the week.

c) I have only a vague recollection of starting
   this quiz.

*Allocate 3 points for As, 2 points for Bs and 1
point for Cs.*

Totals

3 – 5   Congratulations on
reaching the ripe
old age of 200.

6 – 7   You may think you are
old but you are
really young at heart.

8 – 9   You have all the
attractiveness and
attributes of a youngster.
Are you sure that you are an oldie?

Seduction lines for geriatrics

"Excuse me, were you smiling at me or have you just forgotten your false teeth?"

"When I look at you my pacemaker starts thumping."

"If I put my teeth in will you give me a snog?"

"That's a sexy red dress you're wearing. I can almost see your ankles."

"I love your wig. Is it made from genuine rat hair?"

"Are you dancing or are you just feeling a bit wobbly?"

"Kick start my walking frame and I'll take you on a trip to heaven."

"HEY BABY! LOVE THE WAY YOU MOVE!"

Wrinkly power

By virtue of your advanced years you have become a fountain of knowledge on positively everything.

It is now your duty to impart this knowledge to the unsuspecting, more ignorant younger generation. Whenever possible tell doctors, chefs, electricians and anyone else how to do their jobs. Repeatedly ask if they know what they are doing and criticize constantly. By encouraging them in this way they will develop high self-esteem and an increased fondness for their elders.

Oldies' maxim on youth: Youth is expert in everything and experienced in nothing.

"THE ADVANTAGE OF GREAT AGE, HUGE WEALTH AND
COMPLETE OWNERSHIP IS THAT YOU CAN SAY ANYTHING
YOU LIKE, YOU BORING YOUNG FART."

You know your memory has started to go when...

... you have déjà vu about events that happened five minutes ago.

... you start enjoying TV repeats.

... you keep meeting interesting new people – in your own home.

... you finally find what you were looking for but you have forgotten why you wanted it.

... you get a big surprise when you read yesterday's entry in your diary.

... you forget that you have a dreadful memory.

Memory tips

- Only become friends with people called Bill.

- Introduce everyone as "thingy".

- Label all household objects – BED, TV, FRIDGE, CAT etc.

- When out for a walk, drop crumbs as markers so you can find your way back.

- Have your name tattooed on your hand.

- Have a homing device fitted to your walking stick.

- Choose an easy to remember age, say sixty, and stay that age forever.

20% oldie,
80% spare parts

Old age is a constant battle for survival and should not be entered into without the full combat camouflage of wig, false teeth and walking frame.

"I'm going to the garage for my 10,000 mile service" said Robert to his wife.
"Don't you mean you're taking the car for its service?" quizzed his wife.
"No, I've got so many spare parts I think it's better to be checked by a garage than a doctor."

"Ouch, ouch" moaned Fred "I've got really bad toothache."
"Don't be silly," snapped his wife, "you've got false teeth."
"Well – all my teeth may be gone, but at least I've still got my memories."

"HAIR-PIECE, BIFOCALS, FALSE TEETH
AND A LINE-DANCING FIXATION BUT YOU'RE STILL
MY LITTLE TIGER!"

Some disadvantages of old age

- Your chances of becoming a famous rock star are rapidly fading.

- By the time you struggle out of your armchair the telephone has stopped ringing.

- You often find yourself on the opposite side of the road due to over-zealous boy scouts.

- You wake up in a panic when you see your wig and teeth by the bed, thinking that you are having an out of body experience.

- There is no older generation to blame for everything.

"HEY! I'VE SEEN THIS FORTY-SEVEN TIMES SINCE I RETIRED!"

Spend, spend, spend!

Pension: A fund of money which took years to accumulate and weeks to spend.

Oldies maxim on inheritance: Money left to others is money wasted.

Will: Keep it short and simple, like: "Being of sound mind, I have spent all my money."

How to blow your life savings

- Have a set of diamond-studded false teeth made – even if you have all your own teeth.
- Donate them to the slug preservation society.
- Bury them and create a puzzle so your relatives can spend years hunting for them.
- Have a walking frame crafted from gold.

"I'D LIKE IT SOUPED-UP."

From one old wreck to another...

"I can't go out with you I'm washing my hair – it's in the tumble dryer right now."

"Go away – I'm not interested in becoming your toy boy/girl!"

"I never go out with anyone who is less than 50% original parts."

"I'm sorry, I can't hear you. You must have your hearing aid switched off."

"No, I don't want to dance with you – but my mother may be interested."

"I only go out with people who have deluxe model walking frames."

"Go out with you? My head says yes but my pacemaker says no!"

An oldie's prerogative

Youngsters will gladly give you their seat on the bus – if you give them a gentle prod with your walking stick.

Go straight to the front of lines.
If anyone dares to complain, calmly reply,
"Youngsters have got no respect for their
superiors any more."

Till death us do part

A sure sign of old age is that you never argue with your spouse – you can no longer hear each other.

To celebrate their fiftieth wedding anniversary Frank and Jane decided to renew their marriage vows. The minister asked Jane, "Do you take Frank as your husband and promise to love and treasure him forever?"

"Can I have a few minutes to think about this?" replied Jane. "After all it's a big commitment."

The older you get the louder your snoring becomes. Fortunately your spouse's hearing deteriorates at the same rate.

The grand finale

Despite its lack of popularity everyone tries death eventually.

In the middle of his friend Joe's funeral David suddenly started to laugh. "Whatever is the matter with you?" demanded his wife. "Joe and I had a bet about who would live longest. I've just realized that although I've won the bet, there is no way I can claim the money."

Death can be a real irritation for people who like to plan ahead. It disrupts weeks of planning.

"TIMM... DRANK TO EXCESS ALL HIS LIFE; SMOKED
SIXTY A DAY SINCE HE WAS FOURTEEN; GOT RUN
OVER BY A BUS AT EIGHTY-SEVEN."

Grandparents!
Revenge is thine!

Annoy your grandchildren. Secretly spend all your spare time practising their latest computer game. After you've become an expert casually ask if you can have a try. For the first couple of games act as if you haven't a clue. Then thrash them in every game after that. Announce to their friends how easily you won.

Adorn your walls with embarrassing baby photographs of your grandchildren. Whenever they bring a new friend to visit, slowly reminisce about each and every picture. The humiliation should keep the little pests away for another few months.

"OH MY! I SEEM TO HAVE CRUSHED YOUR HAND-SET!"

Operation Oldie

You know that you're an oldie when you are issued with a gold loyalty card by the hospital every time you have an operation.

"I love your butterfly tattoo. You're so brave to have had that done at your age," Mary congratulated her friend Joan.

"It's not a tattoo," said Joan, "I just asked my surgeon to arrange my latest operation scars in as attractive a way as possible."

Top ten topics of conversation among oldies

1. Their latest operation.
2. Sex or the lack of it.
3. The Cost of Living.
4. Their latest operation.
5. How bad the weather is.
6. Their latest operation.
7. Youngsters have it easy nowadays.
8. Their latest operation.
9. The Good Old Days.
10. Their latest operation.

Seventy-year itch

At the age of seventy, Maria was looking for
excitement and romance. She went to a dating
agency, and after filling in a form describing her
ideal partner, she was questioned
by the agent.

"Maria, don't you think you're
being a bit hopeful specifying your
perfect date as a male model
with curly hair?"

"Maybe... Better
make that straight *or*
curly hair."

"WHO'S THIS THEN? WHERE'S MY USUAL DOCTOR? THAT
NICE YOUNG CHAP WITH THE LOVELY LITTLE BUM?"

Some advantages of old age

- You get that terrifying thrill of the roller coaster – just by using an elevator.
- You can embarrass youngsters by smothering them in sloppy kisses.
- You get to ride at top speed on ambulances.
- You can save time by leaving your teeth to clean in a jar by the bed while you sleep.
- Hair maintenance involves sending it out to the dry cleaners once a month.
- There is no need to observe dining etiquette. Slurping and burping will be silently tolerated.
- Instead of taking your children on day trips, they take you.
- You can fill your house with dolls and comics and pretend they're for young visitors.

"WELL, QUITE A LOT OF ME DOESN'T WORK, BUT MY FACE AT EIGHTY IS A LOT MORE INTERESTING THAN IT WAS WHEN I WAS THIRTY."

Dotty dotage

Surviving old age
is a question
of mind
over matter.
Your mind
stops working
but it really
doesn't matter.

"APPARENTLY NOBODY TOLD HIM WE HAD THE
DINING ROOM DOOR MOVED WHILST HE WAS AWAY
ON VACATION."

Old romantics

An old couple were lying in bed reading, late one night. Sheila turned to Bob and said softly.

"When we were courting you told me that you were my knight in shining armour and would slay dragons to protect me.

Do you still feel like that?"

"Absolutely, my darling. I would risk any danger to protect you," replied Bob.

"And you always said that you would climb the highest mountain, sail uncharted oceans and do anything for me. Would you still do anything for me?"

"Yes of course my dear, I would do anything for you."

"Anything?"

"Anything!"

"Well, be my hero. Learn where the tea bags are and make me a cup of tea."

"I'VE NEVER LOVED ANYONE SO BEAUTIFUL
FOR SO LONG..."

The folly never ends...

Well done. You have reached a ripe old age by good, clean living. You have refrained from over-indulging in partying and late nights. And now? What the hell – go for it!!!!

Oldies' maxim on life: Life is for the old to enjoy and the young to look forward to.

The only downside of being old is that when you play "knock the door and run away" you're now much more likely to get caught.

The hair may go.
The teeth may go.
The memory may go.
But the folly goes on for ever